The Void

Jay Lee

BookLeaf
Publishing

Presentation by *BookLeaf Publishing*

Web: www.bookleafpub.com

E-mail: info@bookleafpub.com

ISBN: 9789357440394

First edition 20223

DEDICATION

I want to dedicate this to my son A.B. Through time and time again he's shown me what true transformation was/is. What it means to be yourself no matter how that looks to anyone else. Dance like nobody is watching, forgive with a pure heart, love as you've never been hurt, and play to your heart's desires. Most of all remember it's okay to be who you are no matter what. To move at my own pace on my own time, no matter what I feel to be true. Secondly, I'd like to thank my mom Kimentha Wright. She's always encouraged me to do what felt right in my heart even if it wasn't the standard. When she found my first poem and it was about things a 14-year-old shouldn't be writing about lol. Then and still, she never urged me to stop writing. When I released my first poetry book she was one of the very first to buy a copy just to say she had it. Thank you for always supporting me, even if my hobbies changed every 5 seconds. I love you.

ACKNOWLEDGEMENT

First, I'd like to thank my Gemini Son A.B. He's shown me it's okay to be angry one minute, feel that, then be happy 5 seconds later. I'd also like to thank my friend MaKayla for pushing me out my comfort zone to do something that requires substantial consistency lol.

PREFACE

The purpose of this book is to free you from the shackles of your current circumstances.

It was with the help of my friends Taylor Brown, MaKayla Guerriero, and Beverly Brock that showed me I am not my emotions. It's okay to feel the shit. Just don't stay there.

Empty

You know that feeling when you're in an open space but you can't grasp for air I mean gasp. Fighting to catch your breath, not knowing what's next. Searching for a match to seek your way out, only there's nobody there. Trying to breathe but there's no air, no matter to fill your lungs. To expunge this feeling of deep pity that sits in your stomach, but you can't seem to release it. Can't seem to be at ease, or searching for something that feels like peace. But is it peace? Or is it just you grasping for the pieces of what used to be your old life? Stepping into the gates of what they call heaven, it feels more like a cemetery. A place where your emotions are buried, your fingers penetrating the soil. The feelings of anger and turmoil fill your lungs and the tears falling from your face water what used to be. A part of me, reluctantly, to touch the parts of me that lie in this space of the unknown. A space where a headstone lies as it states "she was a good woman who loved everyone but herself" or at least I thought that's what it says. Or was it just translation? What my mind read, but what my eyes had seen. From so many people, they told me that the grass was greener on the other side, but here my feelings lie buried in a place that seems unfamiliar. No place to take them home, so I roam to fill this feeling called the void in hopes one day, someone will hear my voice.

Chaos

My mind is running rampant, like a fire with a hidden agenda. Rolling down the hills, like Jack and even Jill. I'm just trying to chill, living below my means, I don't even know what that means, all I know is this thing keeps on pestering me. All these different strings pulling on me like wildfire, Pinocchio I swear if you're asking I don't know. Who I am or where I'm supposed to go. I've got all these connections tied to me, pulling on my energy, bitches wanting to be my enemies, I can never catch a break, even if I plead. Let me take a step back and think things through, the invisible ropes to this thing called life just keep seeming to push and pull. But I gotta push through the bullshit and pull myself together. Like Humpty Dumpty being thrown askew in this weather. Debating whether or not this is a game I wanna play. Sorry isn't enough, if I know things are gonna end this way. But they tell me life is about chess not checkers, but who can I run to when I need love? Who's gonna say, ummm maybe I should check her??? Check on who? If not me, then it must be you. It was you, who used me and abused me. Every time I tried to offer myself, all you did

was refuse me. But waiter, this isn't what I asked
for, as she double-checked your order and said
this is what you asked for…were you ready or
not, cause here I come, I mean came and went.
You spoke the Lord's Prayer but didn't know
what you asked for was heaven-sent. A
revolving door is what you thought this was,
thinking maybe if I push she might pull once
more. Only a fool could ask what's Love got to
do with it, when the only part of my heart that I
gave, you so maliciously broke it.

Insane & Tea

How am I ever supposed to know what is peace if I've never felt it inside of me? A sip of warm tea flowing through my body couldn't even keep me warm enough to soothe this bed of lies. Telling me it's going to be okay, it'll get better. When exactly? When does the world stop spinning on its axis, taking these axes, driving them into this wood to the point of insanity? Insane and tea? Don't mind if I do... something sweet and warm to wash down this platter of lies you feed me. Do you want grape or cherry? I heard the two flavors together tend to marry well. Oh, will you marry me? Is that what you told me or did these bed of lies you fed me, deceive my eyes? You know my eyes are bigger than my stomach, so whatever lies you've cooked up they only taste like sweet dreams. Enough to make me comatose, excuse me Can I get some more of those? You're beautiful, you're amazing, you're wonderful so outrageous? Outrageous? Is that where the rage is? Or were you so busy stuffing me with your lies you couldn't see the pain in my eyes begging you to stop? You saw the tears running down my face, and assumed they were happy tears. I begged you to answer me. Feeling like a hostage in this situation asking to remove the duct tape so I could speak.. only my mother said don't talk with your mouth full it's not polite. So when will it be, spew back out everything you said to me, fed to me, washed it all down my throat like gasoline? As you set fire to the rain, it only further ignited the pain. Only for me to say wait stop do it again, until I heard the siren. Playing all night and wondering, if it was me, or just bad timing.

Hit

Some days it's easy to be here, but not be here, maybe if I stand still enough everything will just appear. Maybe if I stand still enough, I'll Have something to hold. Whether it be a memory or something that's a peace of my mind, the endless thoughts running up behind me, steady reminding me of all the moments I didn't seize when I had the opportunity. Sometimes I tell myself, maybe God saved the best thing for last, but is wanting to know more something I should even ask? Trusting the process seems so much harder when everyone you thought you had can no longer be bothered. Being forced to sit in the deepest pits of my thoughts, praying I don't get lost, and realizing by the end maybe I should ask for help. But at that point, at what cost? An idle mind is the devil's playground, child play if you will, but how do I maintain I childlike heart with all these adult ass bills. Life keeps piling up no matter how much you sort it, maybe if I keep repeating the same mistakes, just like school I'll do better to absorb it. My soul can't take any more damage, from my second-hand antics, feening for the drug they call dopamine just to give me the rush I so badly need, and once it's gone I panic. Breathe in, 4, 3, 2, 1, didn't someone say this shit should be fun, on days like this I feel like I'm the only one who gets it. Stop and give me a moment to breathe, I'm begging you please, maybe if I stay still long enough, I can manifest a life of ease. No, wait that's not what I meant, everything's crashing down, and I don't know where the time went. I stopped for a moment, now it's been 3-4 months and I don't know what I'm doing. I feel like this is an endless cycle of seeing how long I can stay sober from fighting for my next dopamine fix, maybe if I just take a hit, it'll take the edge off of this thing called life even for just a bit. Wait stop! It's been two years, a situationship, and more tears, running down my face praying to God to be my saving Grace from a love that was supposed to give me a high, or was it the abuse just taking the dopamine's place? It seems I can never finish anything but, it's been two years right? That must mean something. I've stayed still long enough to see the damage done to the fruits of my labor. Maybe if I take a rest everything will make sense later. But wait no? Everything is as I left it, swiping my card, now I'm moving too fast and life seems too hectic. So I walk away from my only consistent fix, picking up the pieces and putting out the remaining fires that I lit. Not making sense of what day or what time it is, looked down from the steering wheel just once, and now it seems like my life has been on autopilot. Breathe out, 4, 3, 2, 1, wait the last time I did this it seemed like only the worst has seemed to begun. So let me take this last chance to say, not wanting to wake the beast with a simple dopamine fix, is seeming like it's something that's becoming hard to maintain.

Fire

I just wrote a poem that describes what life feels like living with ADHD and I think that may be the best poem I've written. Sometimes you don't realize how fast life is going when you feel life is on autopilot. I feel like life has been on autopilot since I moved in last year. I have to realize this is my healing season. God had slowed things down so I can better work on myself, take a step back to put out the fires I lit, and allow myself to tend to them. My body is exhausted, I feel like I've been running from the man in the mirror for years. Now I'm having to sit and face my fears, only to realize none of this stuff was as bad as it seems, even those moments where my emotions had me feeling like I was going to burst at the seams. Maybe taking up a hobby would be good for me mentally, some way to release all this anger in a way that doesn't sabotage everything. I see my hard work as a punching bag when it all seems to hurt. Just for it to come crashing down, but maybe that's how I like it. Treating my life like it's a project. I can easily start over, knowing that's not the case. This isn't a race, only time can be the judge to see what all will I have to face. Or am I just saving face? Maybe it's time I took the boxing gloves off, to realize nobody was ever the enemy, maybe it's cause you're that not that girl, or maybe they're just not that into me. Greener is where the grass is on the other side, but wait that doesn't even make sense so I know that must be a lie. Playing tricks on my mind like a Jedi, trying to find the deeper meaning to this thing called life, only to end up 6 feet under, with nothing to show for my efforts but mental strife. Now I've made this hole my home, it feels safe and warm. But I hear things amazing things, but I can't see any of it, the ladder I used to get down here, was merely enough to start a fire with. So how do I get out of this hole I've dug so deeply? Do I start to pray and ask God for what I need? I'm begging you please, save me from my transgressions, I mentally can't afford any more lessons. I've loaned out every single part of me, and now I have nothing. Just footsteps that have roamed my heart, only to help me finish something I could never start. Start within myself, I'm begging for your help, send anyone to help me get out of my own personal hell. 4:34 on the clock but what's the deeper meaning, just take my hand and show me what you've got. Being given a second chance at life is something I'll never take for granted, being able to come up from being underwater, is something I've never thought I'd be able to handle. Everything seems so much more peaceful now. Only to realize God never allowed me to lead myself astray, he just knew allowing me to sit in the hole I dug was better that way.

Abyss

There are so many days I wish I never met that man.
Days I look in the mirror and don't recognize myself.
I get life happens, shit changes. But fuck. I feel like
he fucked my head up. Like on good days, he's the
fix my soul craves. I know it's unhealthy but I can't
help myself. Being around you is like my sense of
heaven when it's really hell. My heart feels numb at
the sight of your name. Releasing you feels like a
pain I wouldn't wish on anyone. I feel like I'm one
breakdown away from needing the 12-step program.
But how can I accept, you were only supposed to be a
lesson and not a forever love? I'm tired of replaying
you in my mind like an outdated show, that my
senses crave to be reshown. To be stimulated by your
lies, and soothed by the downs. Only cause I know
it'll come back up. I'm tired, my soul is tired, and I'm
mentally tired. I do not adore or strive to have a love
that makes me feel sick to my stomach. As the boat
rocks, the crash of the waves feels like a thrill, the
anger, the adrenaline, the sadness, the flare. The light
fills the sky as my soul calls out for help. My soul is
crying to be seen, to release me from someone that
was merely a demon of his own kind. Nothing I'd
ever seen before, it's like the monster the kid tells
you is under your bed, only to gaze and see nothing
on the floor. A wolf in sheep's clothing, his claws
embedded into my soul, as my eyes fill with fear,
begging to be let go.

Pinocchio

I am not the toy that you can just pick up when you're ready to play. Performative actions that mimic as though I'm on stage. The spotlight you placed me under, only puts me under pressure, no more no lesser, these diamonds can't be created when I'm out here stressing. The lack of mentality, your inability to receive clarity on what you want, vs what you need. I am the seed that you planted, but you refused to water. Nobodies at fault, not even your daughter. But how can you show her how a man's supposed to act when you can't even seem to face the fact if you're not benefitting from it, it's not love? When you can't even seem to go beyond, let alone above. The bar is set so low, that even diamonds under that type of pressure can't form. You can't expect me to be the tree that bears the fruit you need, when it was me, the seed. Or did you forget that you planted me?! No, you forgot to water me as much as you do your expectations. If you poured as much energy into what you did to manifest me, maybe I'd bear the fruit that was needed to provide you with a sense of clarity. Sense of peace, sense of mind. Only for you to remove the fog off your mirrors to see what needs to be left behind. Let alone what's gone, cause once I cut these strings, you'll understand when Pinocchio said "I'm a real boy".....

Grief

I want to start off my dedicating this poem to someone I met, named Nate Vagrant. This was originally spouses to be a poem, much like a skit between us two. So as I finish this last line today, this closes the door to the many questions that come with grief.

Nate: "There is no beauty in grief, only scars we are now all burdened to keep".

Jay Lee: "Waking up wishing it was all a dream, now that life you once lived isn't what it seems. They say the grass is greener on the side, but at times like this, I wish heaven had a hotline. Looking to the sky praying to God for a sign, hoping this pain isn't infinite or a plan of the divine. You see now my drunken thoughts are scattered, trying to evaluate what pain is mine. Trying to focus on the positive, drunken walking a straight line. At the rate I was at, it only seemed like the highway to hell. But, someone once said, it's a chance I'll take, baby I'll stay, heaven can wait".

Nate: "I dream of the day, where we can all just be left to be, and all find our peace".

Jay Lee: "Nothing comes to a sleeper but a dream, you can't visualize these things, when panic attacks constantly wake you from your sleep. Fighting for an outcome that feels unseen. The only way to keep going is up, to reach for the stars and shoot for our dreams. See things for what they are and not what you want them to be, once you reach that point, herein lies the state of peace. A sense of knowing that everything is okay, everyone's in the right place, only God knows when the things you dream of will come into play."

Nate: Why Lord, am I forced to watch my loved ones become everything they loathe and hate? I yell why lord, this pain has robbed me of all my faith.

Jay Lee: All of your faith? Or all of your fate? They say misery loves company but that's not my place to say. That's not my place to stay, not a place to call home. Some days when I'm forced to go within, I'm seeing my heart isn't a place to call home. I asked you again, so when are you coming home? I'd rather you tell me if this isn't where you want to be. If that's the case so be it I'd just rather leave. Leaving where I stand also means, relieving myself of the boundaries I set. The line I drew only merely being a stop sign before you keep moving forward asking yourself so what's new? Just for you to cross them again, I take you back again? No, not this time, you may be moving on God's time, but I won't allow you to waste mines.

Floating

Feeling my fears flowing like the ocean, taking over my soul, this shit feels like coercion, I'm sorry I meant cohesion. These falling must be a reason, you know they say everyone's either in your life for forever or a season. Reasons like seasons are like throwing salt on a wound, just to turn around and expect healing. But what was I supposed to do, when you were the only thing I ever knew? It's complicated, elated, this love is outdated, you would've sworn this love was in season the way we swore that we made it. To another level, only to be introduced to new devils. Take me to the promised land, where all the false promises seem to land. Upon deaf ears, ringing ringing, my spirit tuning out your lies. It was only to my surprise, the reason I couldn't hear was that I was embedded with lies. Pillow talk on satin sheets, calling it fabricating, no love could've been worst, even then I couldn't take it. Take me to places I'd never been, floating into the sea of your lies, calling it the abyss. You're telling me if I hit it once, I can hit it twice, cause you swear you never miss…an opportunity to claim what was never rightfully yours. So next time maybe you'll have better luck shooting for the stars.

Dancing With the Devil

Not only did you punish me, but you also confused me. Did you want a friend with benefits, just a friend, or someone to date? How was it you could hurt me while searching for me in other women? Were you running from me or running from what I brought to the surface? What I pulled from under the rug? The things that made you think? So was I in turn the REAL villain in your story? Or was I the hero who made you see who the real villains were? Did I remove your ripped cape only for you to see the man in the mirror and see you had become the villain in everyone else's story? You were too busy bleeding on those that wanted to love you. Everyone was bad, nobody was safe. Life was no longer about living, it was about surviving for you. But you added crystals and resin to paint this perfect picture as though the masterpiece hadn't been created from broken glass. Everyone saw the gold, while I saw the cracks and the scars. There wasn't enough money in the world that could hide who you truly are. Not a chain, not a smile, not a piece of fancy clothes…Could hide the pain from the story your eyes told.

Sail

I realized it was never that she didn't know herself. There were parts of her that she had yet to discover, wounds that she dare not open. You see the character she portrayed was never a character. It was simply her trying to find her way amongst a life that did not celebrate both parts of her. She sought out leaps and bounds to find the missing pieces that fit her puzzle. Only to embark on a journey where she would meet different people that had those pieces. Gaining battle scars, fighting relentlessly, searching for this person whom she thought to be. All while an extended piece of her, watching from afar as she embarked on this journey with her. This wasn't something she was fully aware of. Had she known she would've left writings on the walls of her soul, so that when this piece of herself stared deeply into her soul. She'd know and understand that, in the eye of the beholder, lies a story to yet be untold.

H2CO3

I'm learning to make peace with my inner chaos. Rather than fighting to breathe I deeply inhale as I allow the water to course through my lungs. My body already being 75% water how much could it hurt right? It's no different than the tears that fall down my face. Feeling these deep emotions that engulf me. A wave if you will. Rising and falling. I can either rise or fall with it. Or allow it to consume me as though I belonged to it. Allowing these emotions to take me outside of myself was only a mere moment to show how small my existence is, but how big my impact can hit. Reaching from underwater hoping to catch a moment to breathe, only to be pulled back under by my ancestors and the powers that be. Telling me to stop fighting what has already been written for me. It was never meant to be either you sink or you swim. The only way for me to wade through this pain is to accept it is now a part of me. But it is not my whole being. It is simply something I was given to experience and release. As I come to terms with this, my breathing reaches a low peak, the tears have dried, and my anger is slow to peak. What felt like it was ages underwater was only a matter of minutes. To think had I kept fighting, I wouldn't be here to live through this. So next time you try to fight the emotions that have come to engulf you, remember, what is only a few minutes can claim years of your life until you let go of the resistance.

Free

I'm learning what it feels like to be free. What it feels like to only worry about my happiness and what that looks like for me. What does it feel like to have your cup so full, it feels like a warm hug when the sun touches your skin on a cold day. Free to me is having freshly shaved legs on satin sheets, while I lay in bed listening to my favorite song on repeat. Free to me, feels like gathering with friends, laughing, smiling, and sharing stories. With no sense of care or even worry. Free to me, feels like living a life where my triggers no longer have a hold on me. I don't have a voice inside my head telling me who I should be. Free to me, is speaking my truth, without worrying about if there will be a passive penalty. Facing judgment for who it is I choose to be. Free to me, is wearing bright colors on an overcast day, as I do not rely on the sun upon to bring me the shine, it's simply what I become. Free to me, is the freedom to make mistakes without skepticism or fear, this will be something I won't ever want to experience again. Freedom to enjoy my life, my mistakes, my lessons, without strife. Not having to look back and regret the things I did. Because I know

I am simply aligning with the life, I choose for myself. Free to me, is hearing bells, sleigh bells, wedding bells, as a reminder that peace and happiness are not far out of my reach. It's a sign what I crave the most, is closer than I think. Free-dom to me is waking up and knowing, God made it a priority, again, to choose me.

Crave

I want to know what love tastes like on a Sunday afternoon. I want to know what love smells like when I roll over and smell the lingering scent of your cologne. I want to know what love feels like when, when you pull me closer. I want to know what love sounds like when I'm in the kitchen and hear the sound of your keys turning in the door. I want to know what love sounds like, hearing you say I love you just because it's Tuesday. I want to know what love looks like when I see you saging my space as I prepare for my day. I want to know what love feels like when you see me meal prepping. Gathering all my necessities, standing next to me, basking in the smell of my perfume, as I hear you take a deep breath and say, you smell so heavenly. I…want to know…what does love taste like when I sit down for our favorite meal, smell like when I take your grandma's favorite peach cobbler out of the oven, sound like as I hear you scream with such joy that your favorite team won, feel like when you grab my favorite blanket and lie it on me as I fall asleep, look like when I see you reading our children a bedtime story….I want to know what does the love I crave look like, smell like, feel like, taste like, sound like, when im loved by the right one.

Traits

My toxic trait is I fall in love with the idea of you. I don't pay attention to the red flags, cause to me, they're only a cautionary tale. Maybe you should do this, maybe you should do that. But there is nothing that urges me to leave before things get bad. Angel numbers telling me, new beginnings are in store, and there are better things out there if I just shift my perspective. So I did, I allowed myself to be loved, see love, taste love, and feel love…in a way, I didn't know existed. But what fucking sucks, was the way you twisted it. I think you should do this for me, granted it was the fault in our stars, silly me to think the stars aligned. Telling me this love was something divine, I could not see past my own two eyes. I was blinded by what I thought love should look like. It smelled good, tasted good, and felt good. But so does the right drug. The right drug coursing through your veins, your body, your brain. It will have you wanting more. At least that's what I thought. But, just like cocaine when the love is pure, it's hard to put down. Everything around you seems, still and silent, like there's nobody else around. A love like this shouldn't be painful. I shouldn't be gasping for breath after screaming at the top of my lungs for you to understand the words that I am speaking. Why is it I have to repeat myself 5, 6, 7 times? When you heard after the 2nd, I should not be repeating myself AGAIN after the 9th. 999, maybe that's a sign, it's time for me to close this chapter and put down the pen. A love that felt like this, should've ended. No love lost, no love gained, only a broken heart that now needs to be mended.

Transition

When you have gifts that live inside of you, that are thousands and hundreds of years older than you, it can feel as though finding connections is redundant. You no longer move out of your way to seek those that speak this ancient language of your soul. The seeds you carry have been given to you, by ancestors that know this land from top to bottom. Everything you do, every move you make, every thought you think lies within your DNA. The answers to the questions you seek course through your veins. As the blood that runs through you is the spirit of all knowing. While knowing, you are a student before you are a teacher. Relearning the magic that is within, but having a sense of remembrance as though you've done this before. Seeing and realizing much of what you know, is no longer folklore. The random glimpses of light, the shadows out the corners of your eyes, are merely spirits and pixie dust or those that exist in another realm. They say, around Halloween the veil is thin. But, doesn't that only apply to those who can't see what's already within? The gifts that keep on giving, clairvoyance, medium, psychic abilities, all wrapped up in one perfect bow? Just for me? They feel more like parting gifts, as I shed from the person I used to be. Now I'm growing into a sense of this new person, who just so happens to be me.

Cautionary Tale

I was asked which do you feel is stronger fear or love? Most will respond with love because as we all know it conquers all. But fear stops love. Love cannot always overpower fear. Fear is the wall that appears to be in your way only to find out that wall is you. Wanting to tell that person how you feel only for fear to whisper what if. You sink back into the place you tried so hard to climb out of. To finally have the courage to speak up for yourself only to hear "that's not how you feel, it's you". To have those you care about the most tell you how you feel doesn't matter. In fear, they too will feel how you do. Do you see? How fear can spread? How it can make you tear another person's world down just as quickly as they brought you into it. How it can dismantle everything you once knew and had confidence in. Fear is paralysis in a physical form manifested from something that was once mental. Taking its time creating blockages in spaces where love had grown and harvested only to be burned down by the insecurities of those who are not secure within themselves. Now, tell me again how love is stronger than fear.

Release

Broken glass lay upon my feet, staring in the mirror only to see 15 more fingers pointed back at me. Steam clouding the mirror of my inner judgment. Wondering why nothing seems to be clear, even to my wonderment. I say sticks and stones may break my bones and words can never hurt me. So explain to me why no matter what I do, why must the truth cut so fucking deep. They say, hurt people, hurt people. So be careful who you bleed on. Sometimes there is no amount of I'm sorry, I didn't mean it. That can help stop that bleeding once you've cut someone else. Hurt people, hurt people. But I despise. You see hurt people only hurt people when there is something that can't seem to realize. May it be that even the third eye, can't realize, what lies, even when you wanna take the pain away from those eyes. You can't be every man's savior, well cause that's God's work. The more I try to offer a helping hand, the more my hand seems to hurt. Even when I was in pain I dismissed that, because I had known, that love couldn't have been in vain. Broken blood vessels were exposed from the shards of glass in the mirror I refused to see. As those same 15 fingers, 15

hands, reached. For my savior, for my help, for
me in their time of need. Now it is me who
stares back, at those who are no longer bleeding.
As I was offering that helping hand you had time
to tend to your wounds. While I was still so
busy, being in a state of bliss to see you happy
floating in the abyss. Watching you in the foggy
mirror realizing your eyes no longer tell the
story they once told. Now that the fog has
passed those real eyes, began to reveal real lies
of those told by the hands who pointed all ten
fingers at me while the others begged for me to
grab their hand. So now I must cut ties with the
man in the mirror. As it was my lack of
judgment, who couldn't see it was all just my
fear. My fear of being alone, not having a single
place to call home. So as I roam into the places
of people's empty hearts and try to make it my
own. Only that wasn't their intention from the
start. It was them who wanted me to help them
paint this perfect picture. Then once everything
is as it ought to be, they tell me I think that you
should probably leave. For it was my blindness
that allowed me to believe, I could make a home
in a place where it was nothing but leaves. A
place for me to fall, to place my burdens if
nothing at all. To escape the dangers of the
world, because when real eyes, realize all these
painful lies. You'll see this place, is no place for

a girl to call home. When all she sees is the leaves as a sign, of the place that she once called home being left behind. She will realize, that only real eyes could've seen the pain she forcefully put herself through. Now she can either choose. To be one of those hurt people, who hurt people and allow herself to bleed all over those that want to love her. Or, she can pick up the same shards of glass and face the facts. That, that man in the mirror is no longer coming back. For it was only meant to be a reflection of the things I hated within me. Now, it is your turn to pick up your pieces and face all these endings. Just know when you walk out that door, don't forget to grab your keys. For it will be the only thing you have left of me, as a faded memory, of the girl you once knew to be. Sticks and stones may break my bones, but weapons formed against me shall not prosper. When you go to pull that trigger, know it is your life that is at stake. Cause my locks are changed, I hope the words you were ready to feed me are ready before it's too late. Just know when the time rolls around, I hope you're ready by 8.